KEEPING HEALTHY

Exercise

Text by Carol Ballard
Photography by Robert Pickett

HODDER
Wayland

an imprint of Hodder Children's Books

TITLES IN THE KEEPING HEALTHY SERIES:

• Personal Hygiene • Eating • Safety
• Exercise • Relationships • Harmful Substances

Produced by White-Thomson Publishing Ltd
2/3 St Andrew's Place, Lewes, BN7 1UP

Editor: Elaine Fuoco-Lang

Consultant: Chris Sculthorpe, East Sussex,
                         Brighton & Hove Healthy
                         School Scheme Co-ordinator

Inside design: Joelle Wheelwright

Cover design: Hodder Wayland

Photographs: Robert Pickett

Proofreader: Alison Cooper

Artwork: Peter Bull

Published in Great Britain in 2004 by Hodder
Wayland, an imprint of Hodder Children's Books.
Hodder Children's Books, a division of
Hodder Headline Limited, 338 Euston Road,
London, NW1 3BH.

British Library Cataloguing in Publication Data
Ballard, Carol
    Exercise. - (Keeping Healthy)
    1. Exercise - Juvenile literature 2. Health -
    Juvenile literature
    I. Title
    613.7'1

ISBN 0 7502 4188 8

Printing and binding at C&C China.

Acknowledgements:

The publishers would like to thank the following
for their assistance with this book: the staff and
children of Whitstable Junior School, Whitstable,
Kent.

Picture acknowledgements:

CORBIS 14, Jim Cummins Studio, Inc./CORBIS 9 top,
R.W. Jones/CORBIS 7, Cabaret Philippe 12 top,
Bill Ross/CORBIS 12 bottom, Pete Saloutos/CORBIS
27 top, Tom Stewart Photography/CORBIS 28;
Hodder Wayland Picture Library 6 top, 13 top, 25 top;
Robert Pickett 4, 5, 6 bottom, 8, 9 bottom, 10 top, 11,
13 bottom, 15, 16, 17, 18, 19, 20, 21, 23, 25 bottom, 27
top, 29; WTPix 10 bottom, 22, 24, 26.

The photographs in this book are of models
who have granted their permission for their use
in this title.

Contents

What is exercise?

Exercise is any activity that makes your body work a bit harder than it does when you are just sitting still and relaxing. Some types of exercise, like walking slowly, are gentle and don't make your body work very hard at all. Other types of exercise, such as competitive swimming, can make your body work very hard indeed.

▶ **There are many different things you can do to give your body a work-out.**

You can do some types of exercise on your own or with a small group of friends or family. Playing on your bike or going for a walk is like this. Other types of exercise are more organized and may need more people, equipment and a special place. Team games like football and basketball are like this.

◀ **Team games with friends are fun and a great way to exercise.**

All sorts of people can enjoy exercise! You don't have to be young and fit. Many elderly people are very active and enjoy taking part in different activities. There are all sorts of sports organized for people with a wide range of disabilities. Special athletics events are held for disabled athletes, some of whom achieve amazing success despite their disabilities.

When we exercise, it is not only good for our bodies, it also makes us feel good about ourselves.

▲ **The more you run about, the harder your body has to work.**

Why exercise?

One of the best reasons for exercising is that it is fun! Choose an activity you enjoy and make your body do some work!

Different types of exercise help you to be better at all sorts of things. Some activities can help to increase your strength, others help to increase your speed, agility, flexibility and stamina. Exercising can help to improve your co-ordination so that all parts of your body work efficiently together.

▶ *Stretching and bending in gymnastics makes your body more flexible.*

Exercise is good for your health. It helps to keep your heart strong and healthy, so that it pumps blood efficiently around your body. It helps to keep your lungs working efficiently too.

Exercise is a good way of relaxing. While your bones and muscles are working hard, your brain can 'unwind'.

◀ *Running and sprinting use up lots of energy.*

▲ *Tennis is good for improving co-ordination.*

Your body uses energy all the time, but the more active you are, the more energy it uses. This means that exercise can help people to keep their weight under control. Doctors often advise people who are overweight to exercise to help them lose some weight.

⟨?⟩ Fantastic Facts

Exercise is so important that astronauts use special equipment so that they can exercise when they are in space. They might run on a treadmill or cycle on an exercise bike – but because there is no gravity, their exercises are easier than they are on Earth. Their bones and muscles do not have to work so hard, so their bones slowly become weaker. If they did not exercise, the loss of strength would be even greater.

Dressed for action!

Different activities need different clothes. You can wear your ordinary clothes for some activities such as playing in the park or going for a walk. For others, though, it is important to wear the right clothing.

Clothing

Some activities can be dangerous so it makes sense to wear anything that might protect you. You should always wear a cycle helmet when riding your bike, and also protective pads for knees and elbows when skateboarding or in-line skating. Some team games such as cricket and American football have their own special protective clothing – make sure you wear it to avoid injury.

Jewellery can be dangerous in some activities. Long, dangly earrings can easily get pulled or caught during gymnastics, for example. You can avoid these dangers by simply not wearing jewellery when you are doing something active.

▼ *American football can be very dangerous unless the correct protective clothing is worn. Body pads, gloves, helmets and face guards all help to protect these players.*

Healthy Hints

It is great fun to take part in many outdoor activities, especially on a hot, sunny day. Remember that too much sun can be dangerous, though. Avoid being in bright sunshine at midday when the sun's rays are at their strongest. Put sunblock on all exposed parts of your body to stop your skin burning. Cover up with a loose T-shirt and wear a sun hat or cap to protect your head.

▶ *Always drink water after you have exercised, especially when it is a hot day.*

Footwear

You use your feet for most activities, and so what you wear on your feet is important. Some sports such as ice skating need special footwear. Some sports have special rules about footwear – for example, the length of studs on football boots is carefully checked and controlled. Fashion footwear may look great but is not usually sensible for running and being active in. So think about what you are going to do and make sure you have the appropriate footwear.

▶ *When you are playing sport, make sure that you wear the appropriate clothing.*

Warming up!

It doesn't matter whether you're a track athlete, swimmer, football player or dancer – it is important to warm up before you begin. This means making gentle movements, to prepare your body for the exercise you are about to do.

Warming up does just what it says – it raises the temperature of your muscles. After a few minutes of warming up, your muscles and joints will be warm and supple. If you skip the warm up and go straight into vigorous exercise, you are much more likely to injure yourself.

▲ *Jumping helps you to warm up by making your heart work harder.*

▼ *Whatever sport you choose to do, remember to warm up first.*

Warming up is all about getting your whole body ready for exercise. Gentle twisting around your waist and circling your arms will help to loosen up your upper body.

Stretching exercises help to get muscles ready to move quickly.

After some loosening and stretching, try gentle jogging, running on the spot, jumping and skipping – these all help to make your heart beat faster and prepare your body for more vigorous exercise.

◀ *Stretching helps to warm up your muscles.*

!?/ Fantastic Facts

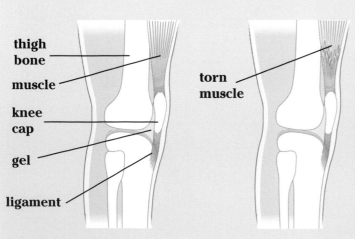

thigh
bone

muscle

knee
cap

gel

ligament

torn
muscle

• Joints contain a gel to help them move smoothly. The warmer you are, the runnier this gel becomes – so the more easily your joints can move.

• When muscles are cold, they are not very elastic so you can easily overstretch them and tear some of the muscle fibres.

◀ *Tearing a muscle is painful. You can prevent this happening by warming up before exercise.*

Stamina, strength or speed?

Different types of exercise are good for developing different kinds of skill. To be good at some sports, you may need all of these skills, while for others you may need only some of them.

► *Cyclists in the Tour de France compete for many days and have to have great stamina.*

◄ *Swimming relies on speed and stamina.*

Exercises such as running, cycling and swimming make your heart and lungs work hard. Exercises like this are good for building up your stamina, so that you increase the length of time you can exercise without getting tired. They also help your body to move more quickly and increase your speed.

Exercises such as weightlifting and yoga may make your heart and lungs work hard, but they do more as well. Weightlifting can help muscles to become stronger. (Be careful, though – weightlifting before your bones are fully grown can stop you growing and developing properly.) Yoga can increase your flexibility and balance.

Many sportspeople combine both types of exercise. This mixture of exercises, together with periods of resting, is called interval training. It is a good way of developing a wide range of skills and making sure every part of you is as fit as possible.

◀ *Yoga is good for flexibility.*

!?/ Fantastic Facts

There are two types of muscle fibres, each good at a different job. Fast twitch fibres are good for short, sharp bursts of activity but they tire quickly and cannot keep working for a long period. Slow twitch fibres cannot give a sharp burst of activity, but they are able to keep working for a long time without tiring. Fast twitch fibres would help a sprinter and slow twitch fibres would help a long-distance runner.

▲ *Sprinting helps to develop your speed.*

Muscles

The muscles in your body work together in groups. Different activities use different groups of muscles. For example, cycling needs strong leg muscles and rowing needs strong arm and shoulder muscles.

Muscle groups

One of the important muscle groups in your body is the abdominal muscles that run in layers up and down and from side to side of the front of your body. Your arms and shoulder movements are controlled by a group of strong muscles anchored to your spine, ribcage, shoulder blade and collar bones. A group of muscles anchored to your spine and pelvis allows you to move your legs.

▼ *Strong muscles help these rowers to row fast.*

Muscles that move your body are attached to bones and work in pairs. When one muscle contracts (gets shorter) it stretches the other muscle. When the stretched muscle contracts, the other muscle gets stretched. By contracting, the muscles pull bones into new positions.

Moving your arm

You can see how this works with your arm: as the biceps muscle contracts, it pulls the lower arm up and stretches the triceps muscle. The opposite happens to lower the arm: the triceps contracts, pulling the lower arm down and stretching the biceps.

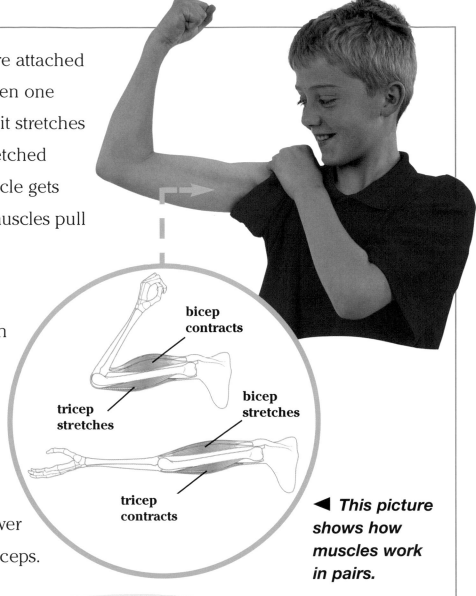

bicep contracts

bicep stretches

tricep stretches

tricep contracts

◄ *This picture shows how muscles work in pairs.*

ᒢᒐᒥ Action Zone

Put a book on the palm of your hand with your arm stretched out in front of you. Put your other hand on the front of your upper arm. Raise the lower arm and the hand with the book on it – can your other hand feel your upper arm muscles moving?

▶ *Follow the instructions on the panel to feel your muscles moving.*

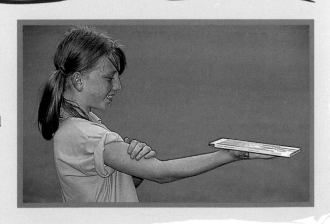

Exercising your heart

Your heart is a very important muscle. It beats every minute of every day, whether you are awake or asleep, pumping blood to every part of your body.

● Muscles need energy to move. Your body gets energy from the food that you eat and stores it in a chemical called glucose. To use this stored energy, muscles need oxygen.

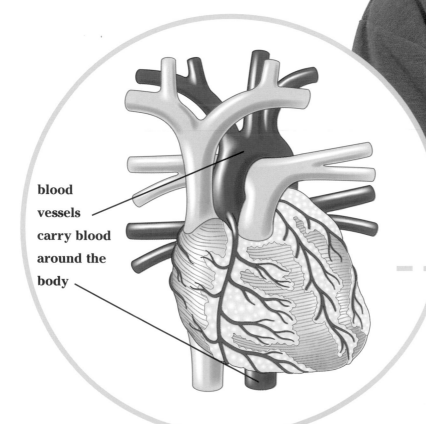

blood vessels carry blood around the body

▲ *Place a hand on your chest to feel your heartbeat.*

• Blood brings glucose and oxygen to your muscles. When your muscles work hard, they need more energy and oxygen – so your heart beats faster to pump blood around your body more quickly. After exercise, your muscles need less energy and oxygen, so your heartbeat gradually slows down until it is back to normal again.

• Doing some exercise that makes your heart beat faster four or five times a week will help to keep your heart fit and strong. If you don't do much exercise at present, try to increase the amount you do slowly – perhaps one or two activities for a couple of weeks and then slowly build up. Try swimming, cycling, running, dancing or ball games.

Action Zone

• Put two fingers gently on your wrist, in line with your thumb bone.

• Can you feel your pulse?

• Count how many beats there are in one minute.

• Now jump up and down for two minutes.

• Find your pulse again and count the beats in one minute.

• Were there more beats this time? Can you explain why?

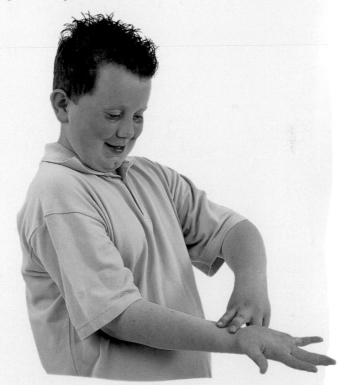

▲ *When you take your pulse use your fingers – not your thumb.*

Temperature control

When your muscles work, they produce heat. This means that your body gets warmer, but you do not just get hotter … and hotter … and hotter! Your body has some very efficient control mechanisms to stop you getting too hot.

Sweating

When your body starts to get hot, tiny pores in the skin allow a salty liquid that we call sweat to trickle out onto the surface of the skin. As this evaporates into the air, it cools the skin down. When you stop exercising and cool down, your skin stops releasing sweat. It is important to drink plenty of water before, during and after your activity, to replace what you lose as you sweat.

▼ *Wearing sweatbands while playing tennis is a good idea.*

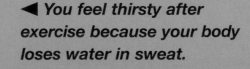

◄ *You feel thirsty after exercise because your body loses water in sweat.*

Keeping cool

Blood plays an important part in keeping you cool, too. When you are hot, tiny blood vessels near the surface of the skin open a little to allow more blood to pass through them. As the blood passes close to the surface of the skin, it cools down. When you get cold, the opposite happens – the blood vessels become narrower so less blood passes through to stop any more heat being lost.

▶ **After you have exercised, your face may look red.**

 # Healthy Hints

When you stop exercising, your body does not stop producing sweat immediately and the tiny blood vessels cannot narrow immediately. This means that you continue to cool down, even though your muscles are not producing any more heat. In a cool climate, you may cool down too much. To stop this happening, remember to cover up with a tracksuit or something similar as soon as you finish your activity.

◀ **Putting a tracksuit on over his exercise clothing will help this boy to avoid overcooling.**

Energy balance

Doing any sort of activity needs energy. Your energy comes from the food that you eat, so it is important to make sure that you eat plenty of energy-rich foods, as well as other foods to help your body grow strong and healthy.

Sugar

Foods such as sweets, biscuits and fizzy drinks contain a lot of sugar. They give you short, quick bursts of energy, but too many sugary foods are bad for your teeth.

Fat

Foods such as chips, sausages and crisps all contain fat that gives you plenty of energy. But it is not healthy to eat a lot of fat.

Starch

Pasta, bread, potatoes and rice all contain starch. These help you to feel full and provide energy for a long time.

Protein

Meat, eggs and nuts all contain protein, which helps to repair muscles and also helps to keep you feeling full. They are ideal, healthy sources of energy.

▼ *Chocolate is energy-rich but it also contains lots of fat and sugar, so try not to eat too much of it.*

You need to balance the amount of energy foods you eat with the amount of activity you do. With too much food and not enough activity you may start to become heavy and sluggish. With too little food and too much activity you may start to become thin and weak. If you get the balance right, you'll be fit and active and have enough energy to do just about anything you want!

▲ *A selection of healthy foods.*

▲ *A tuna sandwich, for example, is a healthy energy-giving snack.*

!?/ Fantastic Facts

Before you exercise, you need to make sure your body has got a store of energy. This is especially important if your activity is going to last for a long time. Sometimes you just need a quick burst of extra energy – sports drinks can provide this, as they contain a lot of sugar that can quickly be absorbed into your blood and carried to the muscles where it is needed.

All in the mind . . .

Exercise is good for your body – and it's good for your mind too. If you are active your body will get fitter, and you'll feel better in other ways too. Your concentration will improve and you'll feel more alert. Exercise can cheer you up too, and you'll feel more relaxed and confident.

► *Active sports such as water-skiing are great exercise for your body and great fun too.*

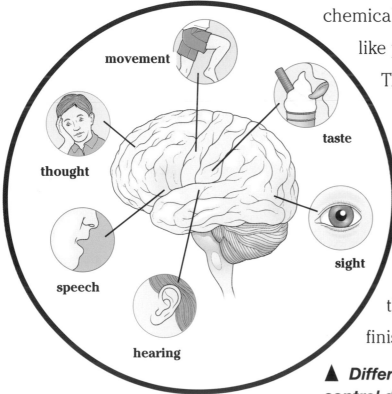

movement

thought

taste

speech

sight

hearing

When you exercise, your brain releases special chemicals called endorphins. These act like powerful drugs inside your body. They can act as painkillers, and they also make you feel happier and more confident. Exercise such as running can make you feel really good inside – people who exercise regularly talk about a 'runner's high', which refers to the good feeling they have when they finish exercising.

▲ *Different parts of your brain control different activities.*

Exercise can help your mind to relax, so you forget about things that might have been worrying you. A relaxed mind and tired muscles can help you to sleep more soundly. Exercise can help to improve your concentration on other tasks such as schoolwork and being more alert can help you to succeed more in other areas too. Improving your co-ordination by doing sports can help you to feel more confident and outgoing.

▲ *Exercise is good for concentration.*

!?/ Fantastic Facts

Exercise can be addictive, just like some drugs. Some people start off just doing a sensible amount of exercise, then they gradually do more and more until they are doing far too much. They become addicted to the endorphins that their brain produces and then it is very difficult for them to stop over-exercising and get back to normal.

◄ *Exercise can help to reduce stress and make you feel less anxious.*

Don't overdo it!

Too much exercise can be bad for your body. Your muscles and bones and other systems all need a period to recover and rest in between exercise. If you do too much, your body has no chance to recover and you may start to feel unwell. Also, too much exercise can mean that your performance actually gets worse rather than better.

► *Athletes need a lot of sleep too, and they make sure that their training schedules allow for this, especially before an important match or competition.*

Healthy Hints

Do you know how much sleep you need? Most adults need seven or eight hours sleep a night, but most children need a lot more – at least ten or eleven hours.

You can easily work out whether you're getting enough sleep:

Count the hours from the time you go to bed until midnight, then add the time you need to get up in the morning.

▲ *Are you getting enough sleep?*

Examples

1. Go to bed at 8.00 p.m., get up at 7.00 a.m. = 4 + 7 = 11 = enough sleep.

2. Go to bed at 10.00 p.m., get up at 6.00 a.m. = 2 + 6 = 8 = not enough sleep.

Your immune system is all the complicated defence mechanisms that keep you well and stop you catching colds and other illnesses. Too much exercise can harm your immune system, so you become more likely to fall ill. Also, if you are unwell it is better to take it easy for a few days until you recover – it's hard for your body to cope with an illness and a lot of exercise at the same time.

▼ *It's not a good idea to exercise when you are feeling unwell.*

Drugs and sport

Some chemicals can help your body to do better at some tasks than it would be able to on its own. Others help your muscles to grow stronger than they would naturally. If you were in a competition, this would give you an unfair advantage over people who had not taken these chemicals. Most sports ban competitors from taking any chemicals like this, such as steroids and epinephrine.

Being careful

Sportspeople have to be very careful because some of these banned substances are found in ordinary, everyday medicines such as cold and flu remedies. They must read the packet carefully and check all the chemicals to make sure they are not taking any banned substances.

▲ **Never be tempted to take drugs to make yourself look different or perform better. As you grow up, keep exercising – this is the best way to keep fit and look good.**

Some young people think that, by taking some of these substances, they will grow stronger and better than their friends and rivals. This is a really bad idea – don't ever be tempted to do it! Some of these substances can have very nasty side effects, and may actually stop your body growing and developing properly.

Be yourself

Let your body grow naturally and be pleased that your skills are the result of your own hard work, rather than produced artificially by chemicals.

◀ *Remember to be proud of your body. If you exercise and eat healthily you will look and feel great.*

\!?/ Fantastic Facts

The people in charge of most sports regard taking banned substances as a very serious offence. Scientists have developed some very sensitive tests that can detect minute amounts of these substances. At a major competition like the Olympic Games, sportspeople are tested at random. Anyone found guilty of taking any of the banned substances can face very serious penalties, such as being banned from competing in their sport for the rest of their life.

▲ *Winning feels great, especially when you put all of the effort in yourself.*

Avoiding accidents and injuries

Whatever type of exercise you enjoy, you need to be careful. Remember always to wear the correct protective clothing for your activity. Accidents and injuries can happen easily but can often be avoided by taking just a few safety precautions.

Going out

If you're going out, make sure an adult knows where you are going, who you are going with and when you expect to be back. That way, if you don't get back on time, somebody will know where to look for you and where to send help.
If you are going to be out when it is dark, try to wear reflective clothing.

On the road

If you are walking, remember to stop, look and listen before you cross a road. If you are cycling, make sure your bike is checked before you set out, and remember to follow all the rules of the road.

▼ **Wearing a helmet when riding a bike will help to protect you if you have an accident.**

Whatever sport you play, there are rules that should be followed. Many of these are for your own safety and that of the other players. You should try hard to follow them, so that everybody avoids injury.

Think of others

Think about other people who may be using the same facilities as you. Try not to do anything that could hurt them or cause them to feel unsafe in any way. This is especially important if there are younger children around.

▲ **Stretching will help to keep you injury free.**

 # Healthy Hints

Just about everybody has suffered from cramp at some time. It can be very painful, even if it only lasts for a few seconds. Cramp happens when part of a muscle that you can usually control suddenly contracts and does not relax. Rubbing the affected area can sometimes ease the pain. Dehydration can increase the likelihood of getting cramp, so make sure you drink plenty of water.

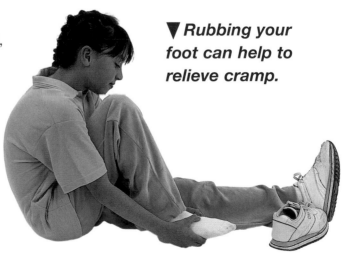

▼ *Rubbing your foot can help to relieve cramp.*

Glossary

abdominal to do with the front of the body, between the ribs and hips.

agility how quickly you are able to move and respond.

biceps the muscle at the front of the upper arm.

blood vessels the tubes through which blood travels around your body.

collar bones the bones at the base of the throat, above the ribcage.

contract get shorter.

co-ordination how well different parts work together.

dehydration losing fluid through sweating.

energy the power needed to do work.

flexibility how bendy you are.

glucose a type of sugar that the body uses as a source of energy.

heart the organ that pumps blood around your body.

immune system the body's defence mechanisms that protect you from illness.

joints the places where bones meet.

lungs the organs that collect oxygen from the air and get rid of waste carbon dioxide when you breathe in and out.

muscles the parts of your body that pull bones to allow you to move.

oxygen a gas in the air that every part of your body needs to work properly.

pelvis the bones that make your hips.

pore a tiny hole.

pulse your heartbeat.

relax become looser.

ribcage the bones of your chest that protect your heart and lungs.

spine your backbone.

stamina how long you can keep doing something before getting tired.

sunblock cream or lotion that protects you from the harmful rays of the sun.

temperature a measure of how hot or cold something is.

triceps the muscle at the back of the upper arm.

vigorous energetic or hard-working.

Other books to read

Fitness for Kids: Strength, Flexibility and Stamina Training for Young People by Simon Frost (Connections, 2003)

Training and Fitness by T.J. Miller (Usborne Publishing Ltd, 1998)

Keep Fit by D. Orme (Longman, 2002)

Muscles (Look at your body) by Steve Parker (Franklin Watts, 1997)

Exercise by Judy Sadgrove (Raintree Steck-Vaughn, 2000)

Why Should I Get off the Sofa and other questions by Louise Spilbury (Heinemann, 2003)

I can't believe it's yoga for kids by Lisa Trivell and Peter Field Peck (Hatherleigh Press, 2000)

Useful addresses

Sport England

16 Upper Woburn Place

London

WC1H 0QP

Tel: 020 7273 1500

Fax: 020 7383 5740

email: info@sportengland.org

Index